All Creation
and the
Isles of Shoals

All Creation
and the
Isles of Shoals

Peter E. Randall

Down East Books
Camden, Maine

To Dr. John Kingsbury
and the memory of the Rev. Lyman V. Rutledge

Page one: The Gosport Church stands over the Star Island Conference Center buildings.

Title page: Foggy afternoon, Appledore island.

Page six: Star island, from Appledore.

Right: The Gosport harbor bell.

Contents

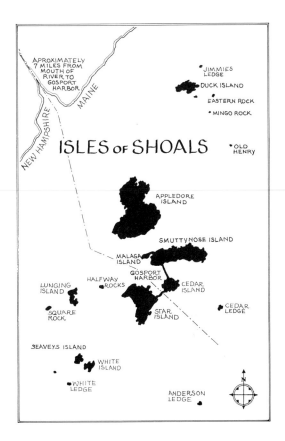

Preface

FRED MCGILL, historian of the Isles of Shoals, likes to tell the story of the old woman from Kensington, New Hampshire who, when hunting for a lost item, would often exclaim, "I've looked over all creation and the Isles of Shoals!"

For her, the islands were a special place removed from the rest of the world. It is the same way that I feel about the Isles of Shoals and one of the reasons why this book was produced.

Straddling the Maine-New Hampshire border, ten miles out in the North Atlantic Ocean, these islands have a lengthy human history and yet they retain a wild, natural beauty accented with native and exotic birds, wild flowers, deep green seaweeds and some of the lushest poison ivy to be found anywhere. For the most part, man has treated these islands carefully, perhaps not purposely, but the result has been the same. A rambling hotel, the stone church, fishermen's cottages and the stoic lighthouse enhance rather than detract from the natural beauty of the Shoals.

These rocky outcrops, remnants of mountains shaped by three million years of erosion and scraped by the glaciers of the Ice age, are small enough so that one is always aware of being on an island. Yet they have enough size so that one can find a place to be alone. A journey to the islands for almost any length of time almost demands that the visitor set aside a period for contemplation. Few who come to these islands for more than a few hours leave without commenting on the changes, whoever subtle, that occur to them during their stay.

Here, without highways, fast food restaurants and a host of other irritants endured on the mainland, one feels closer to more important elements of life. The salt air, the steady winds and the ever changing ocean form the background for the intellectual climate of Star and Appledore. Here the mind and the spirit can soar as high as the gulls, recharging the batteries of life to meet the requirements of mainland living.

The idea for a photographic book on these islands was developed about 1974, the year that Aristotle Onassis attempted to build a mammoth oil refinery on Durham Point, New Hampshire. The necessary off-shore terminal for supertankers was to be located at the Isles of Shoals. Much concern was focused on the impact of the industrial complex on the entire Seacoast but I believed that as harmful as the refinery itself would be to the mainland, the off-shore terminal would forever change the Isles of Shoals.

It is ironic that this marvelous off-shore resource called the Isles of Shoals has generally been ignored by those people who have greatest access to it. While travelling to and from the islands on the *Viking Queen,* I am constantly amazed to see friends and neighbors from the Seacoast on board making their first ever visit ever to the islands. In lecturing about the Shoals I meet many old timers, natives of the seacoast and inland New Hampshire, who have never been to these islands and who have little conception of the character of the place.

New Hampshire's local and state officials would make the decisions about the refinery and if it was impossible to bring them all to the islands, I proposed to bring the islands to them in the form of photographs. Grants from the New Hampshire Charitable Trust and the New Hampshire Council for the Humanities, backed by the Audubon Society of New Hampshire, got my photographic project started. Additional support came from the Shoals Marine Laboratory and many other individuals.

Fortunately, the oil refinery died like a dinosaur, sent packing by many hard working citizen's groups, the members of the Durham town meeting and the New Hampshire legislature. Threats to the islands continue though, and partly to offset the hype of industrial developers and partly because I wanted to show the beauty of the islands to those who couldn't visit them as I can do, the book project has continued.

Since 1974, I have spent countless hours on the Isles of Shoals, visiting every island, photographing, lecturing to adult and students groups, conducting photographic workshops and just contemplating. It has been time well spent.

I am not a genealogist but I feel certain that my ancestors came from the islands. The early history of the Shoals is filled with the name Randall and my more recent ancestors are natives of the New Hampshire seacoast. It seems quite likely that my affection and concern for the Isles of Shoals are stirred by those of my name and family who lived here from the 1600's until the 1870's.

Acknowledgments

This book has been made possible primarily because of the support and encouragement given to me by Dr. John Kingsbury, founder and past director of the Shoals Marine Laboratory. Without his cooperation, it would not have been possible to visit the islands and to have a place to stay during the extended periods necessary for photography. Many laboratory staff members and students have shared Dr. Kingsbury's enthusiasm for this project and their assistance has been immense.

I am also grateful for the assistance and cooperation given to me by the following people: Lenny and Beth Reed, Edward Warrington, Rodney Sullivan, Fred McGill, Rosamond Holt, Robert and Roberta Jorgenson, Mary Louise Hancock, Bill Humm, Jean Hennessey, Bill Brownell, Tudor Richards, Bill Finney, Charlie Tucker, Betty Phinney, Ed Dumaine, Bob Meadows, Ken Olson, Tim Shaw, Carl Randall, Woody Foss, Mr. and Mrs. Philip Fowler, Dominic and Rachael Gratta, Susan Faxon Olney, Ollie Hewitt, David and Edith Pearson, Art Borror, Chris Morrow, Fred Perkins, Betty Lockwood, and Fred Bavendam.

My family has given strong support to this project and I appreciate their willingness to share my affection with a group of islands.

July 1979
Hampton, N.H.

About the Photographs

The photographs in this book were taken with Nikon and Canon cameras and lenses. For most of the bird portraits, I used a 1,000mm mirror Nikkor lens, a piece of equipment that allowed me to get optically close to the birds without disturbing them with my physical presence. Other pictures were taken with a variety of 28mm, 55mm macro and 80-200mm zoom lenses. I used Ektachrome 200, 160 and 64 speed film, also Kodachrome 64, Tri-X and Plus-X films.

Most of the bird photographs were taken from a blind constructed on Appledore and moved into position on rocky outcrops overlooking the thickets where the birds nest.

These two small houses on Star island remain from the days when the island supported a year around population. Between the houses can be seen Smuttynose island and beyond is Duck island.

A Brief History

SITUATED TEN MILES out in the rugged North Atlantic Ocean, the group of nine small islands known as the Isles of Shoals has had an impact on New England history and culture that is vast in proportion to the mere physical size of the islands. The most important fishing and trading center of northern New England in the 1600's and later a place of inspiration for writers, musicians and artists, the Isles of Shoals has attracted the famous and little known, the adventuresome and the humble, the bold and the meek for nearly four centuries.

No one knows when white men first visited the Isles of Shoals but it seems likely that European fishermen came to these waters in the late fifteen hundreds. Cod were so abundant that some historians believe the name of the islands is a reference to the teeming "schools" or "shoals" of fish.

Champlain was the first to mention the islands in a journal he kept during a 1605 voyage along the northern New England coast but the most famous of the early explorers was Capt. John Smith. He was so impressed with this section of New England that he named the archipelago Smith's isles. That name didn't last perhaps because the islands had been called the Shoals long before Smith arrived in 1614.

In his 1616 "Descriptions of New England," Smith wrote, "The remarkeablest Iles and mountains for landmarks are these . . . Smyths Iles are a heape together, none neere them, against Accominticus (Mt. Agamenticus) . . . a many barren rocks, the most overgrowne with such shrubs and sharp whins you can hardly passe them; without either grasse or wood but three or foure short shrubby old Cedars . . .

"And of all foure parts of the world that I have seene not inhabited, could I have but the meanes to transport a Colonie, I would rather live here then any where . . . ."

Smith's belief in the potential of the islands was to be proven in just a few years. Although Smith himself was unable to return, others with the same adventuresome spirit read his words and took his advice.

By the time of the first mainland New Hampshire settlement at Odiorne Point in 1623, there were houses and other accouterments of the fishing industry already standing on the off-shore islands. Eventually (the date is unrecorded), when some fishermen began to winter over on the islands, a permanent settlement developed that was to endure until the 1870's. By the mid-1660's, the population was about 600 and for a number of years the Isles of Shoals was considered the most valuable colony in northern New England in the minds of the English.

Fish was the source of its wealth and Smith recorded that even an average fisherman, with a single hook and line, could catch up to 300 fish per day. Considered larger and finer than fish caught off Newfoundland, the cod were taken ashore, cleaned, split, salted, then placed on stages called fish flakes to dry. The Shoalers devised a special curing process termed dunning and the resulting "dunfish" were esteemed as the finest dried fish produced in the world. For many years the market price for dried fish was quoted as of the Isles of Shoals. Even in the early 1800's, when the industry had declined, Shoals' dried fish brought nearly four times the price of Newfoundland fish.

The early political history of the islands is lengthy and involved. For a number of years the Shoals was an international outpost — a colony with no leader, laws, or allegiance to any country. Eventually the English claimed this area of New England and from 1619 to 1635, the islands and most of the land area of New Hampshire and Maine were under the control of the Laconia Company, a trading company established to foster new settlements and develop the abundant natural resources. For many reasons, the company was unsuccessful and when it was dissolved in 1635, the lands under its control were divided into what became the provinces of New Hampshire and Maine.

The boundary between the two provinces was extended south from the mouth of the Piscataqua river through the middle of the Isles of Shoals. The islands we know today as Duck, Appledore, Smuttynose, Malaga and Cedar were granted to Maine while Star, Lunging, White and Seavey's became part of New Hampshire.

With the collapse of the Laconia Company, the Massachusetts Bay colony began to expand its political influence northward. By 1652, both provinces and the islands acceded to the control of the Puritan colony to the south. During these years, the islanders petitioned the Massachusetts Bay colony to become a separate township. The petition was finally granted in 1661 and until 1679, the township of Appledore was responsible for the local affairs of the islands in both provinces. In that latter year however, New Hampshire became a separate royal province under the presidency of John Cutt, a Shoals native and prosperous Piscataqua region merchant. The southern half of the islands then came under the control of New Hampshire officials.

During these years, most of the islands' population was on Appledore and Smuttynose. About 1680, when the Massachusetts colony, which still controlled Maine, imposed a harsh tax, most of the families on the Maine islands simply moved across the harbor to Star island to avoid the taxes.

For most of the next 200 years, the center of population and activity was Star island. Its town of Gosport was established in 1715 and named for a village not far from Portsmouth, England. The island town elected its own officials, kept records and even had a representative in the state legislature although sometimes the Gosporters had difficulty filling that position.

During the middle 1600's, some of the richest men in New England lived and made their fortunes on Appledore island, but by the turn of the century, as mainland settlements began to grow and develop, the prosperity of the Shoals declined. Fishing continued but the day when the fortunes were made by Shoalers was over. In 1767, the population was 284 and when the Revolution began, the new government forced the evacuation of the islands because the loyalty of the independent-minded Shoalers was apparently in question.

The village of Gosport never really recovered from the evacuation. A few people did return to Star island and Smuttynose enjoyed a brief resurgence in the early 1800's under the Haley family. For the most part however, the returning Shoalers were those who were unable to adjust to life on the mainland. They were fishermen and not inclined to be farmers. For about 100 years prior to 1872, the little village struggled along, poor in money and spirit. Impoverished, given to excessive drinking of rum and not

An old turnstile frames the Gosport church on Star island.

13

particularly concerned with many of the social mores of the day, including marriage, the Shoalers became a rather peculiar people with a dialect and a manner of living uniquely their own.

Missionaries, first supported by mainland parishes and later from the Society for Propogating the Gospel Among the Indians and Others (read Shoalers) in North America, came to the islands as early as 1637. The parish was always a difficult one but after 1800, the responsibilities multiplied. In that latter year, the population was only 112, "including solitaries," according to Gosport Town records and most of them "in a state of great poverty and wretchedness, and to draw from the humane every effort to affort relief."

The population continued to dwindle through the middle 1800's and the end came in 1872 when the owners of a proposed resort hotel brought out most of the remaining residents. In that year the history of the village as a permanent settlement came to an end.

While Gosport was dying as a community, Appledore was in the midst of perhaps the islands' most romantic era. In 1839, Thomas Laighton, a promising young Portsmouth businessman, became the lighthouse keeper on White island. He had purchased several of the other islands in that year and he hoped to reestablish the fishing industry while manning the lighthouse. He succeeded, but as a hotelman, not as a fisherman.

Laighton brought his wife, Eliza, small daughter, Celia, and infant son, Oscar, to the lighthouse with him. A year later another son, Cedric, was born. Although the children spent most of the next decade on the isolated island, their parents gave them a sound education which was accented by the every changing environment where they lived. Celia, in particular, learned to observe the many moods of nature. Her perception of the natural world observed from the tiny island became the basis for her later fame as a writer.

Initially Laighton bought and operated the Mid-Ocean House on Smuttynose. Eventually he developed plans for a larger hotel on Hog island, which he renamed Appledore. An early partner in this venture was Levi Lincoln Thaxter who fell in love with Celia, marrying her in 1851 when he was 27 and she 16.

The commodious Appledore House opened in 1848 and it was an immediate success as one of America's first summer resorts. Celia and Levi summered on the island but usually returned to the Boston area for the winter. During the time away from the islands that she loved, Celia wrote long letters to her family who stayed on Appledore year around. Her poem, "Land-locked," written in 1860 and sent to Cedric, found its way to the editor of The Atlantic Monthly and was published in 1861.

The poem was well received by the New England literary

community and Celia soon became a respected author. Her Boston literary friends, charmed by her personality as well as her writing, began to visit Celia during the summer on the Isles of Shoals. For a quarter century, until her death in 1894, Appledore island and the hotel were the favorite summer gathering place for the leading artists, musicians and authors of the day. To be invited to spend an afternoon or evening in the parlor of Celia's Appledore cottage in the company of Lucy Larcom, John Greenleaf Whittier, Sarah Orne Jewett, Thomas Bailey Aldrich, Charles Henry Dana, James Russell Lowell and others was an experience to remember forever.

With the apparent success of the Laightons, businessman John Poor secretly bought up property on Star island and in 1873 he opened the large imposing Oceanic Hotel. It burned to the ground after three seasons but, using several smaller boarding houses on the island, Poor rebuilt a new hotel, still in use as a conference center on Star island.

The Laightons eventually acquired the Star island property too but by the turn of the century, Thomas, Eliza, Celia and Cedric having died, Oscar was left to carry on the hotel business alone faced with increasing competition from mainland resorts and the high costs of maintaining the island buildings. Oscar eventually sold all of the family's holdings on the island but he remained a perennial fixture on Star

island summers for many more years. He died in Portsmouth in 1939 at the age of 99.

Appledore's romantic era came to a close in 1914 when the hotel and several nearby associated buildings burned to the ground. As so often happened on these islands, however, another influence, another spirit, was bringing to life a new era in the history of the Isles of Shoals.

In 1896, Thomas Elliott and his wife spent part of the summer on Star island and he conceived the idea of relocating a summer religious conference from The Weirs on New Hampshire's Lake Winnipesaukee to the Shoals. The first session was held the following year and by 1916, the Unitarian and Congregationalist programs had become so successful that the Star Island Corporation was formed by these denominations to buy the island and its buildings to make a permanent summer conference center.

With the exception of the World War I and II years, conferences for young people, adults and family groups have been held there ever since. A newly organized arts conference, bringing together professional and lay musicians, artists, and writers, evokes memories of the days of Celia and her friends on Appledore.

Dr. John Kingsbury, who had visited the Shoals in his youth, returned for a week in 1966 to lead field trips into the intertidal environment of Star island at the request of one of

the family-oriented conferences. Dissatisfied with certain trends in marine education at other centers, and immediately aware of the biological richness of the Shoals islands and surrounding waters, he arranged with a number of colleagues at Cornell University to offer an introductory course in marine science at the Shoals. This course was presented initially in the conference center buildings on Star island during the brief period between the end of spring semester classes and the opening of the hotel's facilities for the regular conference season.

From the beginning, this effort looked forward to the opportunity to move across Gosport Harbor into its own full-season facilites on Appledore island. Sufficient funds had been raised by 1971 and a long-term lease signed with the Star Island Corporation to allow the beginning of construction of new facilities on Appledore and the renovation of the deteriorated cottages remaining from the Appledore House days. This was an undertaking of unusual difficulty because most of the island had been abandoned, and subjected to the degradation of weather and vandals since the end of the second world war.

The first regular Shoals Marine Laboratory class occupied the not-yet-finished buildings on Appledore island

(opposite) Monument on Star island commemorates Capt. John Smith's 1614 visit to the islands. In the background is White island.

in 1973. From these beginnings the Laboratory, sponsored by Cornell University and the University of New Hampshire, has grown to an institution offering a variety of credit courses to students from colleges throughout the United States. The Laboratory also presents a number of brief, general and specialized non-credit programs for alumni and the general public during its annual season from May to September.

Proximity to major population centers at Portsmouth, Boston, and Portland, and to the home campus of the University of New Hampshire at Durham, and facilities meeting the supply and transportation needs of the Laboratory have been important to its development. The off-shore location assures unpolluted ocean water, freedom from the mainland's distractions and a diversity of marine plants and animals nearly impossible to duplicate on any other stretch of New England coast of comparable size.

If the study of marine science on Appledore and the emphasis on religion and philosophy at Star provide the steadiest influences on the Isles of Shoals today, then it is only a continuation of the major elements in the lengthy history of these islands. The first settlers were catchers of fish, soon joined by fishers of men and this mingling of the practical and the philosophic which has been part of life on the islands for nearly 400 years seems destined to continue.

Star Island

STAR ISLAND is the most visited of the Isles of Shoals. During the summer months, the island hums with the activity of week-long conferences sponsored by the Unitarians and the Congregationalists. Established for "religious, educational and kindred purposes," the Star Island Corporation owns the island and maintains the buildings which include the Oceanic Hotel, the Gosport meeting house, a number of old buildings, some of which date back to the year-around residents, and several newer stone buildings, the latter reminiscent of an old English village.

This island is named for the many points that extend from its shores like the flashes of a twinkling star.

About 90 young people, nicknamed "pelicans," staff the conference facilities, working for the summer as cooks, waiters and waitresses, chambermaids, bell hops and maintenance personnel. The management staff includes college professors, clergy and laymen, many of whom return to the island summer after summer.

(opposite) Aerial view of the islands with Star in the foreground, Cedar at right, then Smuttynose, tiny Malaga, Appledore and, top right, Duck island. (right) The Viking Queen approaches the Star island dock.

In addition to the religious conferences for individuals and families, Star island offers arts and writing programs, a week long conference on international affairs and the Institute on Religion in an Age of Science. Approximately 225 people can be accommodated at each conference.

For details about programs offered, write: The Star Island Corporation, 110 Arlington Street, Boston, MA 02116.

During the conference season, which extends from mid-June until late August, the excursion boat *Viking Queen* makes three round trips daily from Portsmouth bringing supplies, conferees and day visitors. One hundred people, on a first come, first served basis, on the Queen's 11 a.m. cruise only, may get off at Star and spend three hours on the island. The snack bar, book shop and a guided tour are offered to visitors.

The Viking Queen is the main transportation link between the islands and the mainland.

(this page) The porch of the Oceanic hotel on Star is one of the prime gathering places on the island. (overleaf) Views of Star's buildings photographed from the church tower. Most of the white buildings date from the 19th century while the stone ones are newer.

The old ice house has been converted to an art center.

(above) The bell on the hotel porch tolls changes in the daily schedule. (above right) Choir practice in the church.

(above) Fred McGill, the islands' unofficial historian, awakens conferees each morning with a bit of poetic whimsey extolling the virtues of the day's breakfast. (above right) Speakers and discussion groups covering a variety of subjects set the intellectual climate on Star. (right) Star's relaxed atmosphere is conducive to impromptu discussions.

The Gosport church, circa 1800, is the focal point of activity. The obelisk, lower right, commemorates the Rev. John Tuck, *a missionary who served Star for 42 years until his death in 1773.*

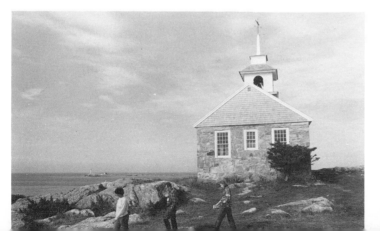

(above) Summer house and cemetery in winter. (left) Newer stone buildings continue the architecture of the old church.

27

White and Seavey's Islands

WHITE ISLAND LIGHT has been of service to mariners since it was first constructed about 1820. Rebuilt during 1859-1860, the present tower rises 82 feet above the ocean and its 170,000 candlepower light can be seen up to 21 miles. The four 36-in. Fresnel lenses provide a flash every fifteen seconds and during foggy weather, the horn sounds once each minute. The facilities were modernized about 1956 and extensive repairs were necessary following the savage storm of 1978 when the light was shut down for several days.

The early history of the lighthouse is filled with tales of shipwrecks and rescues but in recent years the crews have been responsible only for keeping the light in operation. Currently, a three-man crew, on rotating two-man shifts, is assigned to the lighthouse but equipment to automate the light and the horn have been installed and full automatic operation of the facility is expected soon.

Celia Thaxter lived here as a child and her early experiences on the six-acre island helped to shape her appreciation for nature, best exemplified in her "Among the Isles of Shoals," published in 1873.

White and five-acre Seavey's island, both owned by the federal government, are named for former owners.

"Shoals," a friendly Labrador, lived on White island for some 15 years. (left) The powerful light.

29

(above) Inside the walkway that connects the tower with the living quarters. (above right) Some Coast Guardsman with plenty of time painted his conception of White island on the walls of an upstairs bedroom. (right) Coast Guardsmen serve two-week rotating shifts.

30

(left) Inside the lighthouse tower. (below right) Giant waves sometimes shake the entire rocky island. (below) This boat and boat house were destroyed by the rugged winter storm of 1978. Many other Shoals' buildings were damaged and the lighthouse crew was evacuated.

ISLES OF SHOALS

Cedar Island

TINY CEDAR ISLAND, connected to Smuttynose and Star by the breakwaters creating Gosport harbor, is owned by the Hall and Foye families, the latter lobster fishermen from Kittery, Maine. This family has fished at the Shoals for six generations. The island probably is named for the "short shrubby old Cedars" mentioned by Smith in his 1616 narrative.

Summer day,
Star island.

33

(opposite) Black-crowned night heron prepares to land amidst snowy egrets and a little blue heron. (left) Cattle egret is one of many migrants seen on Appledore in the spring. (above) Black-crowned night heron.

(clockwise from above) Lobsterman Rodney Sullivan. Gull greets the dawn on Appledore. Gull nest. Great black-backed gull preys on cormorant chick. (opposite) Late afternoon, Appledore.

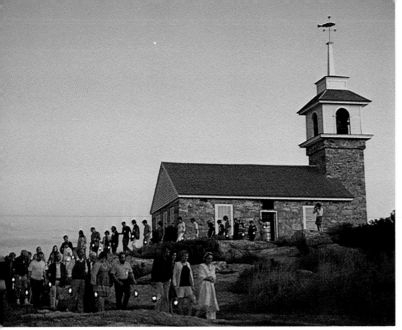

(opposite, clockwise from below) White island. Sunset, Appledore. Common egret, Appledore. (above) A candlelight service is held each evening on Star. (right) A replica of Celia Thaxter's garden has been planted on Appledore.

A February sunrise frames the Gosport church.

Lunging Island

LUNGING ISLAND, sometimes called Londoner's island, was originally used as a trading center for the London Company. Once owned by the Laighton family, its tiny cottage was often used by honeymooners during the hotel era. Now privately owned, Lunging is closed to visitors.

Some seven-acres in size, the island was sought by the oil refinery interests in 1974 as a base for tanker operations.

Duck Island

ELEVEN-ACRE DUCK ISLAND is owned by the Star Island Corporation and managed as a wildlife refuge by the Shoals Marine Laboratory. Access to the island is restricted since casual visitors would have an adverse effect on the delicate balance between the species of birds nesting there.

Only ten feet above sea level, Duck is often completely awash during winter storms. It was named for the migrating ducks occasionally seen on a small pond at the center of the island.

A large colony of double-crested cormorants occupies the southern end of the island and about 1,000 pairs of gulls inhabit the remaining area.

During the fall, winter and spring seasons, harbor seals are found about the island and by April, when the pups have been born, as many as 200 seals can be seen at low tide lounging on the southwestern ledges. Although lobster fishermen place their traps near the shores of Duck island, its many rocks and ledges make it a hazardous place for anyone unfamiliar with these waters.

(opposite) Driftwood, Duck island. (right) Cormorant nests, Duck island.

About 500 pairs of double-crested cormorants nest on Duck island. In the sequence beginning at left, an adult cormorant feeds its young. The parents feed on fish offshore, then return to the nest and stimulated by the pleadings of their young, regurgitate the food into their throats. The young bird then reaches down the neck of the parent to feed. Both adults sit on the eggs and feed the young.

44

Appledore Island

APPLEDORE, largest of the islands, has an unusual history. It was the original population center of the islands with some seventy buildings constructed on its southwest shores but about 1680, when a harsh tax was imposed, the people of Appledore, Maine simply moved across the harbor to Star island, New Hampshire. From 1700 until the 1840's, the fishing community virtually ignored Appledore.

Between 1848 and 1914, the days of the Appledore House, the island was a bustling place all summer with daily steamboats bringing guests, among them the leading art, music and literary figures of the day. By the time the hotel burned in 1914, Appledore's decline was already advanced despite plans by developers to subdivide its 96-acres into 585-house lots.

In 1928, Professor C.F. Jackson of the University of New Hampshire established a summer field station on Appledore, utilizing buildings left from the hotel era. World War II ended this program and for a few years, only military personnel lived on the island. The Coast Guard abandoned their facilities in 1946 and for the next 25 years, only a few fishermen lived on the island and only during the summer months.

When Dr. John Kingsbury came to Appledore in 1971 to begin construction of the Shoals Marine Laboratory there were just three occupied cottages on the south end and seven other scattered buildings in various stages of disrepair.

Four of those old buildings have been rehabilitated by the Laboratory staff and three dormitories, a commons-lecture hall, utility building and a modern teaching laboratory have been built. The Laboratory generates its own electricity, maintains a water system and has its own modern sewage treatment plant.

With faculty members and lecturers who range from professors to commercial fishermen and staffed in large part by college age young people, the Laboratory offers programs from late May until September for college undergraduates and adults. Now under the direction of Dr. John Heiser of Cornell and Assistant Director, Dr. Arthur Borror of the University of New Hampshire, the Laboratory specializes in month-long field marine science programs designed to give a broad view of the marine sciences with a special emphasis on the intertidal zone and offers advanced courses in various areas of specialization. Shorter programs for adults focus on ornithology, coastal zone management and general marine subjects.

The Laboratory is also responsible for the replanting of

Celia Thaxter's famous garden on Appledore. Although Celia was best known for her writing, visitors to the island during her lifetime marveled at her spectacular flower garden. Her book, "An Island Garden," published in 1894 and illustrated by Childe Hassam, provided exact details so that today's garden recreates as near as possible the one that Celia labored in one hundred years ago. Not far from the garden is the Laighton family cemetery with graves of Thomas and Eliza and their three children, Celia, Oscar and Cedric.

Once called Hog island because its shape resembled the back of a pig when viewed from a boat, Appledore was given its present name by Thomas Laighton. There are a few privately owned lots on Appledore but about 90 percent of the island is owned by the Star Island Corporation and leased to the Shoals Marine Laboratory.

Day visitors are welcome on the island during the summer months, although advance notice is required for transportation across Gosport harbor. The *Viking Queen* provides service to Star island but must be met by the Laboratory vessels, arranged for in advance, to carry passengers to Appledore. For more details about the Shoals Marine Laboratory and its programs write (winter): G-14 Stimson Hall, Cornell University, Ithaca, NY 14853 or (summer) Box 88, Portsmouth, NH 03801.

(opposite) Grave marker for Thomas Laighton and members of his family. (above) Two buildings left from Appledore's hotel era. One house, *still privately owned, is slowly decaying while the other, right, has been rehabilitated by the Shoals Marine Laboratory.*

(opposite and above) Two views of Appledore. Opposite, from left, are the Grass Foundation Laboratory and utility building; Hewitt Hall, a dormitory; privately owned Hamilton House; Kiggins Commons; and foreground, Laighton House, the library, lecture hall and small laboratory. Above, from left, are the commons, three dormitories and the Coast Guard building. (right) Palmer-Kinne Laboratory has space for 60 students. The tower was built during the second world war for military observation.

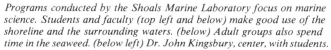

Programs conducted by the Shoals Marine Laboratory focus on marine science. Students and faculty (top left and below) make good use of the shoreline and the surrounding waters. (below) Adult groups also spend time in the seaweed. (below left) Dr. John Kingsbury, center, with students.

(left) Seaside goldenrod, Appledore. (above left) The Coast Guard Building, once ravaged by vandals, has been restored for use by the laboratory. (above) Barnacles, Appledore.

Rodney Sullivan, his wife, Yvonne, and their son, David, all lobsterfish using their home (white house) on Appledore as summer quarters.

(left) Two of the Sullivan boats pass Star island on a misty spring afternoon. (below) The mermaid on the bow identifies Mrs. Sullivan's boat.

55

Lobsters are caught in traps that rest on the bottom of the ocean. Here, left, Rodney Sullivan reaches for a buoy. A winch, center, hauls in the trap, then the lobsters, right, are measured to see if they are of legal length. (opposite) Sullivan chats with a fellow fisherman off Duck island.

Seven of the Isles of Shoals are included in this photograph. The long, narrow island is Smuttynose. Attached to its right end is Malaga. Connected to Smuttynose by a breakwater is Cedar and behind it is Star. White and Seavey's islands are top left while Lunging island and Square rock are top right. (opposite) The grave of Samuel Haley on Smuttynose.

Smuttynose and Malaga Islands

LONG AND NARROW, 27-acre Smuttynose island, owned by descendents of the Laighton family, has the islands' oldest house, almost 3,000 pairs of nesting gulls and a fascinating history. Its name comes from the black or smutty eastern end of the island.

Capt. Samuel Haley's house, built about 1750, has been partially restored by the York Historical Society. Just behind the house is the Haley family cemetery and the graves of fourteen Spanish sailors who perished in 1813 when the ship *Conception* was wrecked during a winter storm.

It was Capt. Haley and his family who tried to revive the fishing industry in the years following the Revolutionary War. They built a wind-powered grist mill, salt works, a ropewalk, a bakery, a brewery and distillery, blacksmith and copper shops and even planted a cherry orchard. By 1819, when Star had only 52 residents, Smuttynose had 26. About the same year, Capt. Haley, Jr. built a breakwater connecting Malaga and Smuttynose. The small harbor and a pier were used regularly by fishermen for many years.

Today, those with private boats often row ashore at the Haley pier to explore the island or to spend the night in the Haley house or another cottage, open to travellers on the island.

One of the most famous and tragic events in the history of the Shoals occured on this island in March, 1873. Itinerant fisherman Louis Wagner believed that a family on Smuttynose had accumulated a large sum of money and one night he rowed out from Portsmouth intent on robbing them. Instead of finding money, he awakened three women in the house and when they recognized him, Wagner killed two of them. The third woman escaped by hiding among the rocks and it was largely because of her testimony that Wagner was apprehended, convicted of the crime and executed.

Malaga island, 2.5-acres in size, is connected to the end of Smuttynose by the breakwater constructed by Capt. Haley, Jr. He found four silver bars hidden in the rocks and used the proceeds from the sale of this "treasure" to pay for the breakwater. His find gave credence to the many stories that pirates hid treasure on the islands. No one has matched Haley's success although many have looked. On foggy nights, the ghost of Blackbeard's girlfriend is said to wander the shores of Appledore, calling softly for her lover's return.

(above) Capt. Samuel Haley's house on Smuttynose has been partially restored. (left) A lady bug crawls on one of the islands' most common plants — poison ivy. (opposite) Ancient stone walls marked the small fields on Smuttynose. In the background are Star and Lunging islands.

Birds

IF THE WATERS around the Isles of Shoals no longer teem with codfish, the skies overhead are increasingly filled with birds. The most obvious are the gulls — nearly 7,000 nesting pairs. The Shoals supports the largest colony in the Gulf of Maine. The herring gull, with about 4,000 pairs on Smuttynose and Appledore and few hundred on Duck and Lunging islands, is the most common gull found along this section of the Atlantic coast. The larger, more aggressive great black-backed gull numbers more than 2,000 pairs with most on Duck and Smuttynose.

Researchers on Appledore have been observing the interaction between the two species for a number of years and at first it was believed that the herring gull was being overwhelmed by the larger gull. Now it appears that both species have increased in numbers. Since gulls have a breeding life of 10 to 15 years and they average nearly one chick raised to maturity per nest per year, one can easily see the reason for the vast numbers of gulls present on the islands.

Despite the impressive gull population on Appledore, other marine birds often excite greater interest. Snowy egrets, glossy ibis and little blue heron, birds considered tropical in nature, are nesting successfully on Appledore at the very northern limit of their range.

A large colony of black-crowned night heron and occasional solitary wanders such as common and cattle egrets give Appledore's New England landscape a tropical appearance during the spring and summer when the birds are nesting.

Dense thickets for nesting sites and nearby mainland salt marshes offering ample food combine to provide ideal conditions for these long-legged, wading birds. Under the protection of the Shoals Marine Laboratory, these exotic birds have thrived.

Duck island has a colony of some 400 pairs of double crested cormorants and on Smuttynose, three to four pairs of black guillmots nest at the southernmost limit of their range. Square rock supports a few pairs of gulls and a small colony of cormorants. A variety of smaller birds nest throughout the islands.

During the spring and fall migration periods, more than one hundred species of birds stop on the islands which are an excellent resting place for the migrants. A formal checklist maintained at the Shoals Marine Laboratory records more than 150 species of birds on Appledore or passing by just off shore.

The Shoals Marine Laboratory sponsors ornithology programs for adults during periods of peak migration and the Audubon Society of New Hampshire makes occasional day trips to the islands several times each year.

Snowy egrets have nested on Appledore island since 1965. They nest (above) in dense thickets. The egrets (right) were nearly exterminated by plume hunters at the turn of the century. (opposite) Adult egret feeds two juveniles.

Three stages in the life of a black-crowned night heron. Young birds, above, born in the spring, appear like this fellow, below right, by the end of the first summer. Adult, above right, is distinguished by long feathers on the head and red eyes.

*Double crested cormorants nest closely together as
protection against the ever-present gulls.*

(above) Mating herring gulls. (above right) Gull chick uses egg tooth to begin the difficult task of breaking out of its shell. (right) Young herring gull chick stays close to its parent.

Great black-backed gulls, left, and herring gulls, below, are staunch defenders of their nests and chicks. The reason for their concern is illustrated on next page.

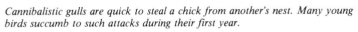

Cannibalistic gulls are quick to steal a chick from another's nest. Many young birds succumb to such attacks during their first year.

Calling gulls can be music or just squawking depending on how early they wake you in the morning. (overleaf) Gull feather on rockweed.

The end of a gull.